Considering Cassandra

The Corgi Series — Writing from Wales

1. Dannie Abse, *Touch Wood*
2. Idris Davies, *A Carol for the Coalfield*
3. Mike Jenkins, *Laughter Tangled in Thorn*
4. *War*, an anthology edited by Dewi Roberts
5. Alun Richards, *Scandalous Thoughts*
6. Alun Lewis, *The Sentry*
7. Tony Curtis, *Considering Cassandra*
8. *Love*, an anthology edited by Dewi Roberts
9. Raymond Garlick, *The Delphic Voyage*
10. Rhys Davies, *Nightgown*
11. Sheenagh Pugh, *What If This Road*
12. *Places*, an anthology edited by Dewi Roberts
13. Leslie Norris, *Water*
14. T. H. Jones, *Lucky Jonah*
15. Paul Henry, *The Breath of Sleeping Boys*
16. *Work*, an anthology edited by Dewi Roberts
17. Harri Webb, *The Stone Face*
18. Geraint Goodwin, *The Shearing*
19. John Ormond, *Boundaries*
20. *Landscapes*, an anthology edited by Dewi Roberts
21. Glyn Jones, *The Common Path*
22. Gwyn Thomas, *Land! Land!*
23. Emyr Humphreys, *The Rigours of Inspection*
24. *Death*, an anthology edited by Dewi Roberts

The Corgi Series  *Writing from Wales*

Tony Curtis
Considering Cassandra
Poems and a story

Series editor
Meic Stephens
Professor of Welsh Writing in English
University of Glamorgan

Carreg Gwalch Cyf.

© Text: Tony Curtis

All rights reserved. No part of this publication may be reproduced or transmitted, in any form or by any means, without permission.

ISBN: 0-86381-707-6

Cover design: Sian Parri

First published in 2003 by
Carreg Gwalch Cyf., 12 Iard yr Orsaf, Llanrwst,
Wales LL26 0EH
☎ 01492 642031 📠 01492 641502
✉ books@carreg-gwalch.co.uk
Internet: www.carreg-gwalch.co.uk

Supported by an 'Arts for All' Lottery grant
from the Arts Council of Wales

Carreg Gwalch Cyf. acknowledges the co-operation of
the author and Seren in the publication of this book.
The Editor is grateful to the writer for his advice in the
selection of these poems and story.

Contents

Introduction 7
Taken for pearls 10
Games with my daughter 11
Key Biscayne 12
Killing whales 13
From Vermont 15
Storm in Vermont 16
Strongman 18
Preparations 19
Jack Watts 20
Letter from John 22
The spirit of the place 25
Land Army photographs 28
My father 30
Poem from my father 32
My father in Pembrokeshire 34
To my father 36
Return to the headland 38
Poem for John Tripp 40
The last candles 41
Lessons 45
Soup 46
Incident on a hospital train from Calcutta 48
Summer in Greece 50
Ivy 51
Letting go 52
Tortoise 53

The Rape of the Sabines 54
Story: HMS Cassandra 55

For further reading 79

Introduction

Tony Curtis was born in Carmarthen in 1946 and educated at the University College of Swansea, where he took a degree in English. He taught at the Barry College of Education and the Glamorgan Polytechnic before it became the Polytechnic of Wales and, in 1992, the University of Glamorgan. In 1994 he was appointed Professor of Poetry at the University where he now leads the MPhil course in Creative Writing. He was Chairman of the English-language section of the Welsh Academy from 1984 to 1988. Among the major prizes he has won are the Stroud Festival Poetry Prize in 1980 and 1981, the National Poetry Competition in 1984 and the Dylan Thomas Award in 1993. The poet contributed an autobiographical essay to *Seeing Wales Whole* (ed. Sam Adams, 1998). He was elected Fellow of the Royal Society of Literature in 2000.

He has edited several anthologies, including *The Poetry of Pembrokeshire* (1989), *The Poetry of Snowdonia* (1989), *Love from Wales* (with Siân James, 1991) and *Coal* (1997). His work as a critic includes *How to Study Modern Poetry* (1990) and *How Poets Work* (1996), as well as a monograph on Dannie Abse in the *Writers of Wales* series (1985); he has also edited *Wales: the Imagined Nation* (1986) and *The Art of Seamus Heaney* (2001). More recently he has pursued his keen interest in the visual arts, editing two collections of interviews with practitioners based in Wales, namely *Welsh Painters Talking* (1997) and *Welsh Artists Talking* (2000), and introducing a new edition of Josef Herman's *Related Twilights* (2002). In 1997 he collaborated with the collage artist John Digby to produce the collection of images and poems for *The Arches* sequence which was later scored by the jazz saxophonist Tim Whitehead and performed at a number of festivals in the UK.

A prolific poet, he has published nine volumes of his own work. His poems are admired for their poise, compassion and note of quiet affirmation which he manages to strike when writing about everyday subjects, particularly his family and the people and places in west Wales, England and America which have meant a great deal to him. He treats the domestic and ordinary with honesty and percipience which enable him to make memorable poems out of what sometimes seems to be unpromising material.

His engagement with the theme of military conflict began in the 1980s after time spent at Goddard College in Vermont where he worked for a master's degree in Fine Arts. Like many people born in the late 1940s, he grew up in the shadow of the Second World War and the Cold War and has come to reflect steadily on what such conflict means. His treatment of this difficult theme might have been bleak if it were not for the sensitivity and dignity which he brings to his subject. Two of his most famous poems are 'The Last Candles', set during the Bolshevik Revolution, and 'Soup', about a prisoner's act of revolt amid the horrors of a German concentration camp, both of which are to be found in *Selected Poems 1970-1985* (1986), *The Last Candles* (1989) and *War Voices* (1993).

The poems in *Taken for Pearls* (1993) and *Heaven's Gate* (2001) represent his most mature work. Technically inventive and with layers of meaning not apparent from a casual reading, they include elegies for friends and relatives, as well as vivid cameos in which a gallery of eccentrics, sportsmen and artists appear and speak for themselves. Each opens up a hidden world and invites us in. There is nothing dense or over-sophisticated about the language he employs, though his images are often breathtakingly bold. Some of these poems have their sources in newspapers (a favourite technique of the poet's), but the people in them spring to life as their humanity is revealed and celebrated. It is this affirmative voice, witty and full of wonder, that makes the poetry of Tony Curtis so attractive and his enthusiasms so infectious.

Taken for pearls

In muddied waters the eyes of fishes
are taken for pearls.

As those two trout, little bigger than my hand then,
taken by spinner at Cresselly on an early

summer's day in the quiet afternoon
before the season's traffic. Only

a tractor in an unseen field
stitching the air like a canopy over it all.

And the taste of them pan-fried nose to tail
by my mother. The sweet flesh prised from

cages of the most skilfully carved bone.
I closed my eyes and she smiled for me.

Games with my daughter

The first clear afternoon of Spring bursts
April's buds and bulbs in the park.
This year when I catch and take her weight
she powers the swing and arcs
from finger-stretch behind my head
to soaring feet-in-the-clouds.
Mothers to our left and right
shrink in their corridors of safe flight.

Our game's revealed the filling out,
the firmer, young woman's stare,
the promise Winter concealed beneath its coat.
Forward and up she splits the sky, each
swing down and back she goes by to where
my tip-toed fingers' grasp can't reach.

Key Biscayne

Sand white, soft and hot,
palms bent over like sheltering arms,
shadows running sand through their fingers,
cool shade.
Sea green, warm soft surf raising white;
and farther out by miles
basking sharks lulled to quiet
by the burning sun.
That horizon ship steams
across your vision:
staring, staring, you watch it
fall over the edge of the world.

Killing whales

Eye sharpening down the line of the cannon:
The crack of the shot
                        high whine
Aching seconds of rope
Spiralling out of the basket.

Slack rope
            and the second, muffled explosion
Tears through bone and blubber.

Whale-back island rising from the deep.
Blow-hole like steam from a boiler.
Wild plunging
                then rising
Resigned to the ship's tether.

Belly over in a slow-motion twist
That could be the discomfort of an itch;
Until that last, low spouting
Like brown water draining a rusty cistern.

Grapple, winch the carcass up the slope:
Out of its element the mass is grotesque.

            Slice
Through the blubber to the red, hot meat.

In the ship's belly white flashes
Pattern the darkness of a sonar screen.

Circling the fleet, whales sing deeply,
Love to the hulls of factory ships.

From Vermont

The snow breathes and stretches the length of the
                                          tall pines.
From dawn, each second of the sun,
bunched snow wrinkles and creases, its layers
tightening around the needles and branches
until the grip closes firm on itself and the load falls
                                          free.

The trees moan inside their snow
(low like the other's dreams after love)
though there is no movement, there is no wind,
nothing to stir the sharp air but walking,
the lungs' steady pump.

Tonight when I phone the line blurs,
marking the distance between us.
You'll be in our bed before my meal is finished.
When I tell you I'm missing you,
that I need you, you smile – 'I bet.'

Love, listen, we are so far
along the way of one another
the hold is firm enough, warm inside cold,
and when it falls it's still wrapped
around our joined shape.

Storm in Vermont

We run at seven through the forest
and the finest rain into
a fresh wood smell coming sappy
and sweet along the path
where last night's lightning
has cleft a pine down its length.

Under that boiling sky
we huddled in the kitchen
and you said:
my skin feels like a cat's.
I said:
the real fear roots in our heads,
it's the insult to reason.
The randomness of the strike terrifies.

Afterwards, with the sound of rain
streaming down the glass,
we all mustered stories of other storms:
on a jetty in Maine
a man and his daughter
burned up, holding hands, each
charging the other;
how some guy's weird chemistry
drew the bolt eight times
until no-one would give him work,
no-one wanted him near.

I hold back and stop. Walk
to the tree and lean my weight against it.
This pine had earthed the whole shock.
Red ants storm over the gashed wood, my hands.
I think of blood let from the flesh.
You've gone on. The pace is telling, still
my breathing jerks the air in and out.

Strongman

A strongman you say.
Home from work would stretch his arms
and hang his five sons from them
turning like a roundabout.
A carpenter who could punch nails
into wood with a clenched fist,
chest like a barrel with a neck
that was like holding onto a tree.

In the final hour
your hands between the sheets
to lift him to the lavatory
slipped under a frame of bones like plywood.
No trouble – he said. No trouble, Dad –
you said. And he died in the cradle of your arms.

Preparations

In the valley there is an order to these things:
Chapel suits and the morning shift called off.
She takes the bus to Pontypridd to buy black,
But the men alone proceed to the grave,
Neighbours, his butties, and the funeral regulars.
The women are left in the house; they bustle
Around the widow with a hushed, furious
Energy that keeps grief out of the hour.

She holds to the kitchen, concerned with
                              sandwiches.
It is a ham-bone big as a man's arm and the meat
Folds over richly from her knife. A daughter sits
Watching butter swim in its dish before the fire.
The best china laid precisely across the new
                              tablecloth:
They wait. They count the places over and over
                              like a rosary.

Jack Watts

squints across a sprouting field,
chews at a leaf, then weighs your crop
to the nearest bag.

Soft cap down to the eyes
and what had been somebody's suit
held by baling cord;
he is pigmented with dirt
as if washing would have drained
away the year's knowledge.

The whole county waits:
in April the Pembrokeshire Earlies come
a stiff, dark green out of the ground.
Jack and his tribe pour
like Winter rats from their cottage.

Jack stops at the stile,
pushes the cap back to the perch of his head,
then walks along a row to what becomes
the centre of the field.
He delivers a potato from the earth,
soil spilling from the web of tubers,
shaking from the clumps.
He scrapes through dirt and skin;
the sweet flesh goes between his leather lips,
a nugget lodging in the jags of his teeth.

He closes his eyes on the taste –
it is the soil crumbling, the crush
of frost, the rain carried in on the sea,
the sweat of planting.

He holds the ridged sweetness to his nose,
between finger and thumb it glistens,
the rarest egg, the first
potato and the last.

Letter from John

It was not for want of think
that I did not rite you a love letter sooner
and this cause I think of you every hour of the day
and every day of the year
and I do love your father to cause he did lend you
                                                the horse
and cart to brought me to the train on Monday.
I shall never forget to remember what you did tell
me when coming in the cart. Oh! Mary Jane
stick to your promise won't you my dear.

I did rive Pontyprydd safe and sound
and I did go strait to the Shop
and when the master did see me he did say
'Man from where are you?'
And I told him that I was John from Maenclochog
coming to work in his shop. The he nowed me in a
                                                minit.

Look you my work is selling cotten
and tapes and hundreds of other things.
They do all call it Happy Compartment
or something, but indeed to goodness
it was not very happy at all to be here without you,
the girl I do love better than nobody
(for all the time I am thinking of you)

Oh, yes you will ask my mother to send my watch
if it is working
cause it will be very handy for me in the morning
to know what o'clock it is.
She do know my directions.

There is a lot of girls in this shop
but not one to match you Mary Jane.
How long you are going to stop
in Mrs Jones' again, Mary Jane,
cause I will try and get you a job at Pontyprydd
to be a Millander.
I will hask Mr Thomas the draper about a position
                                                  for you
for they say he do give very good vittels to his
                                                  clerks.
It will be better by half for you to come
to Pontypridd cause then we will be near to one
                                                  another
for the forehead of Mrs Thomas' shop
and the forehead of our shop
be quite close to one another
and by and by we will marry
is it not my dear?

They say that shop girls do not make good wifes
but you know what Mr Evans the schoolmaster
                                                  said:
'Put a nose wherever you like

and it will be a nose
and put a donkey wherever you like
and it will be a donkey.'
And like that you are Mary my dear.
I believe shop girls will make good wifes
if they have a chance.

Well, I will not rite you a bigger this time
for if it was twice bigger I could never
tell you how I love you.

I send you a piece of Poultry
I did make last night
and if you have not received it
send back at once.

I must finish cause I can hear somebody
asking for hooks and eyes
and your loving John must go forward.

The spirit of the place

Find me in the grass.

Find me in the West Wind.

I am between beats of the waves.
Winters I sleep in the seed potatoes
stocked in the dark.

Spring my sap works through tubers
stretching for light. Earth closes on me like a coat.

My engine coughs across the morning-grey farm.

I flower in the straigth furrows of the angled steep
                                                fields.

I walk the coast path witnessing sun-rise
and fall of globes.

I am the flashing tinsel greed of sky mackerel,
the grey moving of tope deeply beyond Caldey.

I come blackly as cormorant.

With rain I will sweep the litter, rust the cans,
I will take buckets of brine and sluice the piss-smell
from the chapel of St Govan.

I will erase the last scratch of writing,
save that in sand.

My weather eats the oiled guns of Castlemartin.

My surf rides in white, fucks fissures and cave.

I spread my legs in the cliff heather
move with waves.
My cries crack the headland's concrete bunkers,
spike the last war's ghost barrels.

Summers I twist lanes into blindnesses of faith.
I grit through carburettors till they phlegm to a
                                                stop;
my nails slough caravans into ditches.

I turn signs.

I rustle the paper bag dropped in the rabbit warren.

Autumn my dusk stirs mice through gaps;
they lodge in the galleries' ledgers,
shred and nest in the gift shops' trash.

I am the last revolution of the screws
of the last tanker nosing into the Haven;
I hang from the Cleddau Bridge,
stare out to the disappearing sea.

I scupper the moth-ball fleet.

My hands dip into rock-pools. Cool.
Anemones flower and close at my touch.

Nights I breathe Calor Gas.

Gulls are my envoys:
they glide and sweep above your heads,
they feed on your droppings.

There! See! And then!

What have you to say?

Land Army photographs

How lumpy and warlike you all looked,
leaning against the back of a truck,
hair permed underneath headscarves;
in make-up, corduroys, with long woollen socks
– the uniform completed by a khaki shirt and tie.

You are posed in a harvest field:
long wooden rakes and open necks in one
of those hot wartime summers. Fifteen of you
squinting into the camera,
and the weaselly Welsh farmer, arms folded,
his cap set at an angle
that would be jaunty for anyone else.
He's sitting there in the middle, not really
knowing about Hitler, or wanting to know,
but glad to have all those girls
with their English accents and their laughs.

Mother, how young you look, hair back,
                             dungarees,
a man's head at your shoulder.
You girls cleared scrub-land, burned gorse,
eyes weeping as the smoke blew back;
milked cows and watched pigs slaughtered.
You, who could not drive,
drove tractors with spiked metal wheels, trucks.
And once, on the Tenby to Pembroke road,

along the Ridgeway, they had you working flax.
For two days only it bloomed,
the most delicate blue flowers.
Like wading into a field of water.

I see you piling the gorse. Dried spikes
flaring into silver ferns, and smoke
twisting from the piles as the wind comes in
gusts, cool from the sea, the gulls drifting
lazily on the flow.

                And then,
one of them, too steady, too level, becoming
a Sunderland coasting in to Milford Haven:
over Skomer, Skokholm, Rat Island, over the deep
                                    water;
and, though you do not know it, over a man
who is smoking, scraping field potatoes
for the searchlight crew's supper,
who pulls and unpeels the rabbit they have
                                    trapped,
joints and throws it into the steaming stew,
the oil-drum perched over an open fire;
the man who looks up, the man who is my father,
watching the white belly of that flying boat
cut into the Haven.

My father

My father is a shadow
growing from my feet.

This shadow grows from one minute
past the noon of my life
and trails me like water.

My father is mending all fifty-three of his cars.
He works in a garden shed
by the caged light of an inspection lamp.
The red glow at his lips shows constantly
small and fierce like an airliner overhead
or the startled eye of a fox.

Ash falls onto the greased parts
of the dynamo.
He hawks and spits through the door.

His hands and nails black with grease
come out from the old paint tin
he has filled with petrol.
Like rare birds they rise
their plumage glistening and sharp
spilling green and blue and silver.

Those hands that my forehead meets
briefly and shivering.

Those rough hands I run from
like the borders of a strange country.

Poem from my father

The two who spotted her
– approaching but no closer –
come back up the beach like dogs from the waves.

I never thought you squeamish of flesh,
and though your life has been frayed and tattered
by your predilictions for the wrong choice,

you take on the indisputable fact of death,
dealing with the mess, putting on responsibility
                                    like a coat;
your second casual corpse in as many months.

She has fed the fishes
her face.
The rings of her fingers have slipped their flesh.

Belly pregnant with the blue swell of her guts.
They have sucked through her breasts
to the heart's cage.

Six weeks adrift the wrong side of living,
she is something quite other
than wife, young woman, mother.

There's an old blanket you drop over her,
a stone laid at each corner.

Sand could open and swallow her spread body's
$$\text{horror.}$$

Sentry for an hour before the police,
your seventh cigarette beginning to taste;
smoke against a sky tight as a drum.

The sea offers up ourselves to ourselves.
Looking out to the grey island,
you start to hum.

My father in Pembrokeshire

One of those godly days on the Headland,
gorse with the yellow coming to burst,
the tight heather and curled grasses sprung
                              underfoot.

Such days are numbered for you,
we spend our time here like wages.
Precious the slow, awkward breathing,
the laboured talk is precious.

The sand over on Caldey never seemed so bright,
the island stretching empty arms to the west
in that early summer Sunday
before the trade fills the streets and the beaches,
and the noise of the day washes
out from the town a mile or more,
louder than sea.

I have to go further down.
I have to go down to the water.
The way is worn rough and safe;
I crawl to the edge of a chimney shaft.
The sea lies calm as well-water,
green with rocks growing patterns underneath.

To lose myself in the long moment,
drinking in the depth, the abstract shapes.

Back at the top, you say –
Feel my neck –
and the growths blossom along your throat
under my fingers.

Under the sun, the prodigal sky,
there are no healing waters.

To my father

Bellringing was another
of the things you didn't teach me.

How many crooked ladders did we climb?
How many belfries did we crouch in?
The musty smell of the years in the wood beams,
the giant domes balanced to move
against a man's pull.
Stories of jammed trapdoors and madness
in the deafening that draws blood.
Once you rang for the Queen
and I watched
all that pomp ooze into the cold stone of the
                                              cathedral.

I wanted to take the smooth grip of a rope
and lean my weight into it.
I wanted timing.
I wanted you to teach me
to teach my son's son.

Turning your back on that
brings our line down. What
have you left me? What sense
of the past? I could have lost myself in the mosaic
of Grandsires, Trebles and Bobs,
moved to that clipped calling of the changes.

I know now the churchbells coming over the
                                         folded
town's Sunday sleep carries me close to tears,
the noise of worship and weddings and death
rolling out
filling the hollow of my throat.

Return to the headland

There seems no point in angels
or ogres. Now I have no need
for the cartoons of guilt or shame.
The dead go where we send them.
At the crematorium I read 'Do Not Go Gentle'
before the vicar's book freed
your soul or whatever it be that soars
from the husk of flesh.
The curtains purred to their close.
Outside, the long summer of rain,
grey and grey and grey blurred
over Narberth's sodden hills.

It would be easy to construct a myth.
The box jammed under
the baby-seat in the back of the car,
bumping our way up to the Headland.
Early evening. The sea green and flat,
moving and murmuring in the hollows beneath
our feet. Not a cloud shaped, though the horizon
east across Wales is dimming into grey.
The urn is some sort of alloy
like a child's toy, light and wrapped around
what we're told are your ashes.

Not in the sea – says my mother –
he was never a man for the sea –

I step off the path to the slope of rocks
and two rabbits break for cover
from the startled grass.
The stuff shakes out and falls free:
dust, ash on the stones, my shoes.
Stiff-armed, I send the empty tin
over the edge right down to the water.
A jet chalks its line high above the ocean,
pushing steadily away from night.
We turn our backs on a sky that goes on for ever.

Poem for John Tripp

We have filled this church, like a cold, damp barn
perched above Lancashire mills on the edge of the
                                               moors.
Wind that razors through to the bones;
leavings of snow on the hills,
moulded to the underside of low stone walls.

With god-knows what light, the pre-Raphaelite
stained glass records the Whitworth's son and wife:
In Loving Memory – 27 years – 31 years. 1894.
Today is Barbara in her box,
chrysanthemums, the death flowers, arranged on
                                               the lid.

Our third funeral within a year –
this friend dead at thirty-two,
her daughters too young to know what it is they
                                               feel,
like an unseen draught chilling their dreams.
I've had enough of this coldness, of loss.

John, we are under the weight of this thing
And we wol sleen this false traytour Deeth
clench the fist around the pen, we riotoures three:
you and I and the third – our dead friends and
                                               fathers,
on the road, at the desk, looking over our shoulders.

The last candles

The final stage of our journey over
we reached Odessa. So glorious
a scene I think my eyes had never taken in –
the harbour bristling with ships of all the allied
                                              nations.
We were received at the consulate by a young man,
fresh and clean in a crisp English suit.
Courteous and gentlemanly. I had not seen
such a man for four years.

In the hotel that night my dreams were of uniforms
and wounds, but one wound served for many –
thus, a severed arm at Biyech, the lacerated
stomach of a boy in Khutanova, the bloody head
of a captured Turk in Noscov – and then swabs
fell like the first snows of Winter,
the land chill and beyond pain
under its bandages.

For breakfast we were offered good bread and
                                              an egg.
The smell of coffee made me dizzy.

At nine we leave for the harbour. The streets
packed with aimless crowds, though everything
makes way for the *Bolsheviki* in their lorries.
At the harbour gates a man of no apparent rank

holds our papers for an hour.
He has a rifle and a long knife hangs
from his belt. A red band has been clumsily
sewn to the sleeve of his coat.

Some of the Norwegian crew speak English.
My cabin proves small, but warm.
After years under canvas, sheltering in ruins,
nursing beneath shattered roofs,
I am glad to call it home.
Though the place is strange and metallic
after stone and wood and earth.

Doctor Rakhil calls to take me on deck
for our departure.
       Ten years of living in this great land
have brought me to love it.
Though three of those years have been spent in
                            war,
and then this anarchy, this revolution.
I see Odessa under red flags
as we cast off and the engines churn.
I feel everything moving away from me
as if Russia were a carpet being rolled to the sky.
At the harbour mouth Doctor Rakhil
gently turns me from the rail,
but is not quite quick enough.

That night, the sea pressing around me,
I dream of three things –
                         a day
in Moscow, when Nadya and I
were close enough to reach out and touch
the Tsar, and an old peasant
who had crawled through the crowd, between
the legs of the guards, clutching
his ragged petition,
still calling out as their boots struck him.
Nicholas II, Tsar of all the Russias, flickered
his eyes, but his step was the unfaltering
step of a god.
                My first dead man
in the training ward. Grey and small in the
                                    candlelight,
his mouth like a closed purse and what seemed
to be butterflies on his face. Two sugarlumps
to weigh down his eye-lids.

                   And at last, this leaving
Odessa. How in the shadows I saw them –
officers from the front fleeing the chaos of
                                    desertion
and caught by the Reds at the port.
They bound their feet to heavy stones
and planted them in the harbour. Swaying, grey
                                    shapes
I glimpsed from the rail, as if

bowing to me.
The last candles of my Russia
guttering and going out under the black sea.

Lessons

Right up the edge of the pit
The Professor of History taught:

Every tree, every cry
Every tear, every leaf
Each death, each blade
Of grass. Remember everything!
We are scribes – one of us
Perhaps will survive
And be all our future.

The wet, black earth on our feet.
The rattle of bullets in the trees.
The sun jewelling that belt-buckle.

* * *

At Birkenau I saw one of your kind –
He was in the Sonderkommando at the crematoria
Scribbling lists by the light of the furnaces.
I snapped the pencil and tore the paper –
He said nothing.
We made him throw open the doors and put them
                                                                in –
He was silent.
Then we shot him and fed him to the flames.
On my walk back to the barracks
I read his name in the sky.

Soup

One night our block leader set a competition:
two bowls of soup to the best teller of a tale.
That whole evening the hut filled with words –
tales from the old countries
of wolves and children
potions and love-sick herders
stupid woodsmen and crafty villagers.
Apple-blossom snowed from blue skies,
orphans discovered themselves royal.
Tales of greed and heroes and cunning survival,
soldiers of the Empires, the Church, the Reich.

And when they turned to me
I could not speak,
sunk in the horror of that place,
my throat a corridor of bones, my eyes
and nostrils clogged with self-pity.
'Speak,' they said, 'everyone has a story to tell.'
And so I closed my eyes and said:
I have no hunger for your bowls of soup, you see
I have just risen from the Shabbat meal –
my father has filled our glasses with wine,
bread has been broken, the maid has served fish.
Grandfather has sung, tears in his eyes, the old songs.
My mother holds her glass by the stem, lifts
it to her mouth, the red glow reflecting on her throat.
I go to her side and she kisses me for bed.

My grandfather's kiss is rough and soft like an apricot.
The sheets on my bed are crisp and flat
like the leaves of a book . . .

I carried my prizes back to my bunk: one bowl
I hid, the other I stirred
and smelt a long time, so long
that it filled the cauldron of my head,
drowning a family of memories.

Incident on a hospital train
from Calcutta, 1944

At a water-stop three hours out
the dry wail of brakes ground us down
from constant jolting pain to an oven
heat that filled with moans and shouts
from wards the length of six carriages.

We had pulled slowly up towards the summer
hills for coolness. They were hours distant,
hazy and vague. I opened the grimy
window to a rush of heat
and, wrapped in sacking, a baby

held up like some cooked offering from its mother –
Memsahib . . . meri buchee ko bachalo . . . Memsahib take –
pushed like an unlooked-for gift into my arms.
She turned into the smoke and steam.
I never saw her face.

As we lumbered off I unwrapped
a dirty, days-old girl, too weak for cries.
Her bird weight and fever-filled eyes
already put her out of our reach. By Murree
                           Junction
that child would have emptied half our beds.

At the next water-stop my nurses left her.
The corporal whose arms had gone looked up at me
and said, *There was nothing else to do.*
Gangrenous, he died at Murree a week later.
His eyes, I remember, were clear, deep and blue.

Summer in Greece

Each day at noon the Englishman
drives into the sea.
He uses a seven-iron and places the balls
on a strip of carpet which he carries rolled
under his arm from the villa. A dozen
or two small splashes in the ocean.
They sink and cluster in the sand
gleaming like the hearts of opened sea-urchins.

Later, when it is cool, the boys swim out
and dive. They gather the balls –
Dunlop, Slazenger, Titleist, Penfold –
and return to the village. These are eggs
you can't crack or eat. They bounce.
There are no golf courses here.

Some mornings the Englishman from the villa
buys golf balls from the village.
They are cheap and the supply is constant.

Ivy

The choking ivy we lopped and sawed and tore
and one day – yes, in a blast of anger – burned
from the old pear still clings.

As we axed and ripped the tentacles
it slacked its biceps, unclenched its fist.
I climbed and hacked while you
dragged great clumps of ivy to your bonfire.

But high in the thirty-foot summits
clogging this season's hard, sour pears
the last clutch of parched, rootless stuff
worn like a wig still weighs on the tree.

By October winds should have scattered the dead
                                                leaves
and you'll watch me climb again to snap
the final twists of brittle tendril.

At full stretch I shall prise them loose
then feed them down through the bare branches.
And you, my boy, will look up to me with
                                          impatience
like a climber at the bottom waiting for ropes.

Letting go

The trees shake their snow
like a dog at your window.

The world is plant and animal –
it melts, it dies, it falls.

So we make of it art.
Those dry brown grasses in the snow:

the summer's Queen Anne's lace,
old women laying their bones against white sheets.

That gust of wind, the hand
lifts snow dust from the pines.

It powders across the field, turns to
breath in the air. Something to do

with letting go.

Tortoise

They bought you a tortoise and every Autumn your father packed it away in its Winter box of straw in the house-loft. One year in the late Spring, you climbed up to find the box empty. You all searched the grimy space, finding nothing and coming down dirty as sweeps.

Years later, your mother writes that four houses further along the terrace they've found a shell in the loft. Just that. A shell, hard, perfect and whole. Inside, a shrunk ball of jelly.

The image makes you shiver for days, then it lodges in the back of your mind. To travel and come to nothing, leaving behind something shaped, hard and scoured out; an object which no longer holds or needs you, being finished, and what it was always growing towards.

The Rape of the Sabines

That wild dance across the pink land
is a welter of bodies coming out of left field,
a fling of a rape in a hot country where
the legs and the finery of the Sabine women are a
                                          blur,
their over-the-shoulder faces determined on flight.
They yield only in their own country.
Except there is one already caught
in a forced, awkward embrace, her head
thrown back so that her hair touches the ground,
her breasts the fruit of all labour.
Her young, un-bearded Roman looks away –
beyond the flurry of the others,
away to the wide, hot land they must people.
They are already one and the same future.

Ceri Richards, 1948

H.M.S. Cassandra

I picked him up from his bus-stop this side of Cardiff. He hadn't shaved and carried a battered suitcase tied up with string. It was like some debris from a refugee camp, but had a fresh Lufthansa sticker on the side. He had been given the trip to the Berlin Poetry International the previous winter.

'That's the first bloody sky-lark those buggers at the Arts Council have thrown me in years,' he said, 'Probably because no-one else wanted to go.'

I asked him what it had been like. 'So fucking cold it was, boy – a cold city Berlin. If you're sober. Not that many of us were. Full of heavy-jowled, besuited official poets from behind the big curtain.' I hadn't known it was East Berlin.

'Oh, yes, boy, it was the wrong side of the Wall. Or the right, depending on your flag. The commies – Russians, Yugoslavs, Czechs – they're always having these arty jamborees to prove they have real writers. You come away knowing nothing more about real life over there. And caring even less. The stuff sounds like a badly dubbed film from the war over the translation headphones – all tractors, freedom and uncovered Nazi atrocities. Half their lives are spent in profound contemplation on a snowed-in railway station somewhere.'

'You didn't enjoy the trip, then?'

'What? Course I did. No complaints. I cut away from the forums and hit the beer-cellars with this Pole – Eric, I called him – couldn't understand a bloody word. A slice of life though – all grist to the mill.'

All this was in the late seventies and Griffiths would have been in his early fifties; that time when there was a late flowering of the work – those dark bitter poems. Life slurred through broken-down teeth. It was a year or two before that collection *With a Long Spoon* came out; the one that went into paperback and won an award in London. He hadn't made it that big at the time I'm talking of – a couple of books from the Welsh publishers – the odd half-hour spot on t.v. from Cardiff. He was the poet they'd wheel out if there was a nit-picking issue about Wales and culture they thought would fill half an hour. The state of Anglo-Welsh Literature, that mouldy chestnut of the English language being allowed at the Eisteddfod – you know the sort of thing. Sometimes I think that arguing about Welshness is the only thing that makes us Welsh. Anyway, he'd liked some of my stuff in the magazines and we'd exchanged letters and phone-calls. We had never met, though he lived just a twenty-minute drive across the city. He'd been invited to do the Dyfed Music Festival, a couple of readings with music. Well, I hadn't a clue, but a student of mine put me on to a singer who lived down in west Wales and was cheap. The three of us were to do an afternoon in Glanmor and another in the grounds of an hotel between St David's and Fishguard. Two sets of poems, with the singer coming in between to give some relief from the words.

He talked incessantly on the drive down to Pembrokeshire. It was July and the traffic was heavy. I had imagined he'd be cold, keeping his distance, but he talked and talked, mainly about other writers, gossip with a sharpened edge. He couldn't stand Margot Evans, 'that Queen of the salons,' he called her. And then he'd deepen the conversation and come out with something heavy like, 'I write in order to slow the whole thing down – I want to catch death by the balls.' All the time his left hand clutched the passenger door handle as if he thought I was going to turn us over in a package of windscreen glass and blood. I move along a bit, but I've never been that bad a driver.

I think the trouble for him might just have been machines, any machines. There's that poem in *The Collected* – 'the grunts and slobber of cogs and oil' – something like that. He'd got by over the years with train tickets, and the tube when he was on the staff of a paper in London, but he didn't seem at ease with things as personally controlled as a car, or tape recorders, or cameras. 'The tedious inevitability of human error.' Perhaps that's why he was so aggressive on the box; sometimes he'd snarl past the camera as if it were some voyeur who had no business eavesdropping on him. At other times he'd glare directly into the lens like a blood-and-brimstone preacher, right into the hearts and guilt of the pews beneath him. Of course, at other times he could be what Margot called, 'a pussy cat'.

At the St Clears traffic lights I had to brake hard behind a cattle-truck with no tail-lamps and his knuckles went white. He pulled a hip-flask from the inside pocket of his jacket, took a mouthful which he rinsed around his mouth and between his teeth before swallowing. He offered me one, which struck me as odd, but I refused.

When we reached Glanmor I parked the car in the new multi-storey and then called Ralph Dawkins from a phone-box on the main street. Dawkins was our contact for the reading there and had a paper from the Arts Council with his details. Griffiths paced outside the phone-box like a chained, moth-eaten tiger, smoking and picking at the stone-work of the old town walls at each turn. Dawkins told us to call at his restaurant before going up to venue on top of the West Cliff. He warned us against bringing the car; it was a narrow and awkward track, he said, and the weather was for walking, wasn't it? He had a high, whiney voice with an accent that was Lord Cut-Glass, confident, born to lead. Everything that Griffiths hated, in fact, and I feared there would be trouble.

He wheezed and moaned as we walked slowly out of the old walled town and started along the West Cliff road. 'Bloody English settlers. Why can't this Dawkins bloke drag himself away from his money-making to pick up the poets, then? What is he – some sort of sodding English leech?'

I tried to steer him off the subject. 'The Emerald Hotel over there,' I said, 'My old aunt used to wash up in their kitchens every summer. Came in from her rotten little cottage back down the Swansea road. Probably the only time her hands got washed too. She must have ruined a few holidays with what she brought in under her nails.' I began to remember more details of Aunt Annie and would have run through the stories of her wart charming powers and other witch-like behaviour, but we found ourselves outside Long John's, which was Dawkins's place. It was on the first floor of one of the large, eighteenth century townhouses looking back towards the West Beach and the harbour. A man greeted us from behind the till by the door:

'Ah, our poets – so good to see you. And right on time. Welcome to you both. I'm so looking forward to our first poetry reading.'

He was a lanky man with a stiff bearing and a firm handshake that altered the impression which I had formed of him from my phone call. He was a few years older than I, in his late thirties, and I had expected an older man. He sat us at one of the tables with a view and offered white wine from a carafe. We both said we'd eaten before leaving Cardiff, though Griffiths took a round of prawn sandwiches with his wine. Dawkins explained that the cliff-top house had been in his family for years, coming to him three years back when his great-uncle had died.

'I mentioned the temple on the phone, didn't I? The old boy had it built back in the early Twenties – the last of the Welsh follies, sort of. There's a story about Isadora Duncan dancing there. Isadora or one of her followers. He'd certainly bring a string quartet up for parties in the garden. I've been looking for an opportunity to put the thing to use ever since the place came to me. There's a tremendous view from that point. So, finish your wine, gentlemen, and come up and see it for yourselves.' He took off his apron and gave instructions to a waiter. We were due to start at 4.30 and I was getting worried about the singer, who'd not been mentioned. Griffiths wasn't bothered about anything by then. He'd smiled and nodded at Dawkins's story of the Temple, while finishing off the carafe of wine. The last two glasses even encouraged him to muse a little, he began to extol the beauty of the sand, the bay and the old town.

'Imagine what it must have been like before the

Great War, before that waste of young guts in the mud, eh? Under Edward – horse-drawn, tea and tiffin under the parasols, ankles sexy in the waves. Cigars and walking-cane. And then a slow train creaking its way back up the line to Carmarthen. I sometimes think I was born too late.'

I was about to remind him of the stream of broad socialism and dissent that had coloured his writing, but he was mellowing there in the sun that began to shine strongly through the bay window, and I let it go.

The climb up to the West Cliff was a trial. I was pretty well in trim in those days with regular tennis and two young kids to chase after, but the sun had strengthened through the cloud cover and Griffiths had slowed down to a crawl. After three or four minutes he stopped and sank sideways into the hedge, saying he'd had it and why hadn't I used the bloody car? Dawkins apologised, but said that he always walked to the restaurant, as exercise; he also pointed out the pot-holes, which were certainly a problem for cars. He promised to return us to the car-park in his Landrover. 'I'll be done for by then,' protested Griffiths, rubbing at his chest. But, after a long mouthful from his hip-flask, he got back to his feet and we continued. We made another hundred yards or so then cut through a hedge into a large, landscaped garden laid around a low, white house. There were neat shrubs and an ornamental fish pond into which Griffiths hawked loudly and spat. He was looking as flushed as a wino by then, but as we followed the path around the house and down the steps to the Temple he almost broke into a run.

At first I was disappointed. The temple was a mini-theatre along Greek lines, with a semi-circle of stone slabs banked into four rows of seats. The performing area was four or five yards across with a couple of broken doric pillars framing the view across the bay. It was this view which made the place. Over the edge of a wall between the pillars was a sheer drop to the rocks creaming the sea, over a hundred feet below. The curve of the cliff opened up a fine view of the old town. You could see the line of the medieval walls, the harbour and the old fort on the hill. The sky was clear now with just a fleck of cloud remaining to the east.

'Just like postcard, boy. What a place for a reading, eh? Worth that bloody climb.'

Griffiths seemd fully recovered and was raring to go. And indeed an audience had materialised behind us. There were five people: three elderly women who seemd quite happy to be out in the air and talking to each other, a studious, self-contained boy of about seventeen who wore heavy glasses, and a man in his late thirties who had a distinguished air. He was casually dressed in cords and a pullover, but everything about him looked quality tailored, leisure made-to-measure. Ralph was returning from the house carrying a tray with glasses, a bottle of mineral water and a carafe of white wine. He smiled at the audience and introduced the man to us as his brother, Jeremy, who was visiting. 'Do call me Jeremy,' the man said.

'Where's the bloody musician?' grumbled Griffiths, breathing smoke and wine breath into my face. I apologised and began to explain the tenuous nature of the contact, but he lost interest and turned back to the view.

His was in the middle of his third poem when the singer turned up. He finished the verse, paused to glare at the lad, who'd flicked open the catches of his guitar case, then completed his first set of poems. The audience had swollen by this time with arrival of two more elderly women, and then a family of Brummies who'd obviously taken the wrong turn off the cliff path and were too bewildered to leave. Jason, the singer, had brought along four friends, which, at least, made the whole performance seem more credible as an event. Still, I couldn't dispel the feeling of disappointment which the reading was giving me. I read reasonably well, mainly to impress Griffiths, but he, after the rather turgid, committed ballads of Jason's interlude, put everything into his second set of poems. He ended with *Cold Blessing*, which he introduced as a new poem. I thought it was stunning, and one of the women clapped. This was indeed a real poet. The man who'd written that could be forgiven anything, I thought. Then he sat down and the rest of the audience, myself included, clapped. The Brummy father came up and said it wasn't really their line of country, but thank you.

Griffiths signed a copy of one of his books for the women who'd clapped, then Dawkins pointed us up to the house. We were to have refreshments which his wife had prepared. I was thinking it would have better if she had come to swell the audience, but when she entered to serve us coffee all was forgiven. Audrey was an attractive woman, thirty-odd, slim with expensively cut hair and a Laura Ashley summer dress. I felt high after the reading and warmed by the sight of her. I couldn't stop myself staring at the wisp of hair at her neck as she moved around us with the tray. There was a brushing of soft hair under her arms and her face, without make-up was strawberries and cream in the way only Englishwomen can be.

'We were so pleased to be able to put the Temple to good use,' she said. She thought perhaps they might interest the local drama group, and there was the possibility through the Arts Council of a string trio from Aberystwyth.

Jeremy came in with the singer. He said he had

liked Jason's stuff (bland, folksy pathos and concern), and was inviting him to play on his ship at Fishguard.

'Got a yacht, have you?' interrupted Griffiths, mouth full, spraying biscuit.

Dawkins explained that Jeremy, his half-brother, and he had both joined the Royal Navy from school. 'I resigned my commission five years ago, but old Jeremy here has gone from strength to strength,' he said, matter of fact.

Jeremy said to Jason, 'The chaps with me in *Cassandra* would love to have some live entertainment on the bill this evening – we can't pay you, but I can say with confidence that a good time will be enjoyed by all. The Navy knows how to entertain, believe me. Well, what do you say? Are you game?'

'The Queen's Navy never spared the bottle or the grog, as I recall,' said Griffiths, 'Those navy boys were a riot in London in the war. We'd be delighted to come and read.'

Jeremy was shaken. The sailor's eyes flickered twice, quickly and his mouth poised around a show of teeth. But he rode the blow with professional grace, saying poets, almost without hesitation, that, of course, we were included in the invitation. In fact, some of his chaps were keen readers and that a couple of poems might make an interesting interlude in the evening's musical entertainment.

Later, as I drove north towards Fishguard, I said to Griffiths, 'What the hell have we let ourselves into?'

'Take a chance, boy,' he said, 'We've got to be in Fishguard for tomorrow anyway, so why not accept the hospitality of Her Majesty's Navy?'

'No matter how grudging that may be,' I said, 'I mean, do you really think he wants us, too?'

But he was off on one of his long speeches about the role of the poet, the eyes of the blind, a prophet unsung in his own land. How, in Wales, the poet was the natural successor and antidote to the ranting priest. 'You've got to shout, take the bastards on. Otherwise they'll grind you down with their indifference. Because they care only about their cars, and their double-glazing, and their wives's sagging tits. You've got to be outside it all – take it from me. Look to the chances. They're few enough in the grunting banality of this world. Hey, that Ralph's Audrey was a bobby-dazzler, wasn't she? A jolly roger raiser. A high class filly, that one.'

We reached Fishguard around tea-time and I drove down to the harbour to check on the place where the *Cassandra*'s launch was supposed to pick us up. We had two hours to kill and found a cafe. Griffiths didn't want to be bothered with inspecting the B&B place we'd been booked into, but I phoned them from the cafe anyway. Then we walked up and back through the small town with its gift shops and docks smell. Griffiths grumbled at every gift shop – the rock, the plastic beach stuff and cheap mementoes. I remember buying one of those flying disc frisbee things for my kids. Back in the car park I tried to show Griffiths how to throw it. He was quite hopeless and quickly used up all his breath. I was starving, but he said to wait, as the British Navy would be sure to feed us like kings. So, I drove back down to the harbour and parked the car in the grounds of the Hotel Westward, which gave a good view of the quay we needed.

In the bar Griffiths began on pints, several pints. 'They live like kings, those British tars. Last of the Empire. You mark my words, boy, there'll be good grub and a stream of booze.'

I drank a Campari and soda, a literary drink, I thought. And then another two, emptying both bowls of nuts and raisins at the bar to keep me going. I said that life in the services was the last thing that I'd want.

'Oh, of course, not for a family man. And you're too young to have done National Service. That was a game. How many bloody angry young writers have pissed out their memoirs of those glorious chapters of British history – Cyprus, Singapore, Eden, Berlin and Brecon.'

I asked him what his war experiences had been. He finished his pint in a long swallow before explaining that they'd found one of his legs shorter than the other and that he'd been restricted to working as a journalist in Fleet Street for the duration. I later heard a story about Griffith's pal sorting him out a friendly doctor who'd signed him out of the war. That might have been true for all I know. I couldn't imagine that Griffiths's body, even then, would have made a significant contribution to our fight against fascism, and that way, at least, he'd not been wasted like poor Alun Lewis. He went on about Dylan making good out of the war, with scripts and talks and screenplays. He'd seen him from time to time in London. 'Drinking with the smart thinkers – directors, BBC wallahs and the publishing boys. Propaganda was his line, as far as I could see. No bugger's made his fortune out of poetry – except Browning, Eliot and some of the circus-ring Yanks.'

I'd had three or four Camparis by this time and the medicine taste had softened and mellowed. The salted nuts had run out and I was using less and less soda in the drink. I think at this point I went into a long monologue about the vivacity of the Americans. How I'd rather write like Lowell or Plath than Dylan and Watkins. Brought up as a television kid, it was the pop music and films of Hollywood that nourished my imagination: rites of passage that went from Buddy Holly through to Del Shannon and the Beach Boys.

'Different times – different games,' he said, and bewailed the passing of the cinema at its prime. *'Gone with the Wind*, Edward G., Garbo, Lana Turner, *The Cruel Sea.*'

It was past nine and Jeremy had promised a launch by 9.15. We left the hotel bar and at the front door I nearly keeled over. The salt air of the Irish Sea scoured the inside of my skull. It was a slow walk down to the quay side. From there we had a fine view of the ship – metallic grey, the ensign waving at her stern and the glint of brass in the last of the evening sun. The horizon was far and clear, so you felt as if you could have stood on a ladder and seen Ireland. The *Cassandra* looked a fine ship – so fine it made me want to cry. Whether it was the drink, or all those stiff-upper-lip war films dredged up in the mind, I don't know. Most likely it was the drink. But there was strange feeling of potency and significance that she gave off.

'That ship could ride the whole world,' I said.

By ten o'clock the sun had fallen, we had paced the whole quay, and the mystery had all but evaporated. It was getting chilly and there was still no sign of the launch. Griffiths was for giving it up. But a patrolling docks copper came past and proved sympathetic. We got him to radio through to the *Cassandra*. They were awfully sorry. Of course. They'd picked up the singer earlier, but the launch was coming back over in a short while to collect us.

'The bastards don't want us,' grumbled Griffiths. I resisted the temptation to say I told you so; I wanted to reach that ship. I was still high on the Campari and getting a dry, sandy mouth. I wanted to finish the trip.

The launch duly arrived and we were ferried out. And, by god, an officer saluted us aboard as we climbed up the steps at the ship's towering side. This mark of respect obviously tickled Griffiths and he was in high spirits again as we were shown to the Petty Officers' quarters. The singer was finishing of his stint, apparently, and we were to join him in a while at the captain's party. There was no mention of our reading poems.

The P.O.'s were drinking in a room which seemed incredibly small. Four of them slept there and in one corner they had arranged an improvised bar with a fridge, several cases of beer and an assortment of bottles of spirits. They were as bemused as we were at our arrival and the captain's request that they entertain a couple of poets. They'd had worse jobs though, and were a sociable bunch. There was a cockney and a couple of northerners. They'd seen the world and it had seen them often enough. 'It doesn't matter a toss where you are after a while – hot or cold, yellow or pink,' one of them said. I wanted to hear about it all – the Far East and the women and the fights, but Griffiths started on about the beer, which was clearly to his liking. They explained that it was an export brew and their staple diet while at sea. The two cans I got through almost demolished me. I remember being shown down a corridor and a flight of steps to a lavatory. Standing there at the shiny, metal urinal I felt as if all the acid in my life was draining away. The whole ship was metal: metal handles, metal doors, metal walls and ceilings. Warm, grey metal most of it. When I leaned against the bulkhead it felt it would melt. Somehow I got back up to the mess.

'What do you lads do? I mean, what's all this for?' asked Griffiths.

'The defence of our glorious country,' the cockney said, 'We are yer floating weapons system. Missiles. We could take out a ship or a town, makes no difference, at several miles. Just blow the whole fuckin' thing apart. Do you boys want to see the stuff? Think we can trust e'em, lads? Come on then.'

We followed him through a maze of those metal tunnels, clanking down past a small-arms and rifle rack to a locked door. 'Have a butchers,' he said, sliding back a spy-hole. Griffiths pushed forward and thrust himself against the door. 'Take a look in there, boy. There's more heads in there than our audiences.' I pressed my eye to the hole and its glass lens. The room beyond mushroomed out, lit by a low, yellow glow. Ranks of missiles stood in there. They were single, discreet blind shapes in rows stretching for yards. I thought they were a true obscenity. Lines of polished, sharpened weapons, a sprouting of evil, neat as asparagus in a bundle.

On our way back, at the top of some stairs, we were met by a seaman who said we'd been summoned to the captain. We clanged our way after him as he led us up more flights of steps. For me the thing was turning sour, but there was a real shock in entering the reception room, which was brightly-lit and perfectly circular. I felt dizzy and confused, the noise of talk and laughter and the smoke made me want to return to the clean, stark purpose of the ordnance bay.

'Here's our Welsh poets,' said Jeremy, who was wearing a starched shirt, dress trousers and cummerbund. Welcome aboard, chaps. Perkins, get them a drink, would you?'

I was about to say that we'd been kept waiting on the dock and then on board his bloody ship for an hour or more, and had only been picked up as a sort of afterthought, but Griffiths stepped in front of me, shook the captain's hand and ordered drinks. Then I realised that Jeremy was pretty glazed himself and that it was he, not the ship, which was swaying. There was a gauze of socialising noises punctuated by loud bursts of male laughter: it looked like all the other officers were pissed too. Jeremy explained that the *Cassandra*'s forward gun turret had been rendered redundant by the advent of her guided missiles. It had been his idea to carpet and decorate the place, making it a circular reception room. 'Damn hard when it comes to hanging pictures,' he said, and emptied his glass. Scotch and water was the drink to have, but I stuck to orange juice from there on. It was a case of surviving, for the only food left was on a central table, the leavings of a finger buffet which I picked at whenever I had the opportunity. There was a tableau of white-shirted young officers in various states of animation; they lined the walls like a frieze. The only dash of real colour was a woman in a long evening dress.

'There's Dawkins's piece,' said Griffiths, 'What's she doing here? Isn't it supposed to be bad luck or something?'

I turned and focussed on her. Bad luck – who would care? In those surroundings she was a vision of coolness and depth. I half closed my eyes and she was a kingfisher glimpsed through river mist. I breathed deeply and cleared my head. We were side-tracked then by a group of young officers who knotted themselves to us and practised their socialising skills. Luckily, Griffiths had drifted into a mellow phase and responded to them warmly. Why not – drink was flowing and the evening had risen a few notches socially. All was compliments and friendly banter until the door opened and the singer was half carried in between two sailors.

'Sunk without bloody trace my little songbird,' he called across the room, 'What sort of a bloody poof name is Jason, anyway?'

One of the older officers intervened and the strummer and his guitar case were ushered back out of the room. Griffiths launched into a ramble about men and ships: real men and real ships. Then he was striding through a discussion about N.A.T.O. and the Russians with a bevy of listeners, openly filling his hip-flask from a bottle of scotch too. 'Keeping the Great Bear in chains . . . That bastard Stalin was worse than the bloody fascists . . . ruling the waves for freedom of the artist's voice . . . ' He was spouting at speed, on automatic pilot. That's how he managed those famous radio talks, I'm sure: as long as he had an audience, it just flowed.

I think I'd slipped down onto the carpet and was propped up against the hessian of the wall shortly after that. At any rate I was becoming completely absorbed in the scene unfolding directly across the diameter of the room. Audrey Dawkins had her back to the wall and Jeremy was pressing closer to her. Of course, I could hear nothing above Griffiths's performance and the general chatter, but I could make out her lips saying yes and no. She was saying little else, but her face was doing a lot in response to the stream of talking that came from the captain. As the drinks tray came around she put her hand firmly over her glass and he waved the man away. Soon afterwards he put his hand to the curve of her neck. Her free hand came up to cover his, but she didn't brush it away. He held her fingers and she closed her eyes, swaying a little. It was as if I could hear her moaning softly, on a separate sound track. I wanted to be where Jeremy was, but I was miles downstream. I struggled to my feet in order to work my way closer to them, but at that moment Griffiths brought the whole room to a standstill with a bellowing declaration: 'This has been a fine night, a marvellous night! We owe it all to the Senior Service – The British Navy!'

The group around him shouted, 'Bravo!' Then he announced that he would read a poem.

'A poem written this evening. A poem about a war experience that has stayed with me over the years. The story of a seamen who died in the Atlantic.' He took out of his jacket's inside pocket some scraps of paper, unwrinkled them and then read a piece about the death of Jack Cornwall, his eyes closed for much of the performance. It was raw, but fine and stirring. Jesus, I thought, he's magnificent. I never saw him publish the poem, and when I mentioned it the next day, he said it needed much more work. But a few years after he died I came across it again, or most of it, at least. It was in an anthology – Charles Causley's 'Ballad of Jack Cornwall', – which Griffiths had half memorised and half improvised that night. Still, it was a brilliant move and they all loved it. I got to my feet and clapped.

As more people were drawn into the lionising of Griffiths I felt someone nudge against me; it was Jeremy at my shoulder. He seemed supremely stiff-upper-lipped in an abstract way. I looked beyond him, scanning the room, but there was no kingfisher blue dress.

'God, I loved her so much,' he said, as if to himself. I thought he was on the edge of something – the prow of a ship clearing ice.' I can talk to you. Poets. Word-spinners. We met at a ball in Portsmouth. Years since. But she married Ralph. I was in the middle of a long duty, based in Hong Kong. Could have jumped the bloody ship when I got the news. It's a mistake, of course. She knows that now. Did you chaps sense that at the house? I want her to leave him. I would resign the service, of course. Ralph's a cold fish, half-brother. Our father. Audrey should . . . '

'I could see how you felt earlier tonight, when you were with her over there,' I said.

'She's in my cabin. She's there now,' he said.

'Then why . . . '

'But I want the whole thing. I want all of her to myself. Nights and weekends only make it worse. Damn it – she simply must leave Ralph!' He swallowed the last of his scotch and blinked to clear his eyes. 'Thank you for coming,' he said, quite formally. He was standing upright, 'and thank Mr Griffiths.' Then, pausing to say something into the ear of the steward, he walked out of the carpeted gun-turret.

The party dribbled away shortly afterwards, as if the captain's departure had signalled its close. They took Griffiths and myself back up on deck. He was still holding forth as we tottered down the boarding steps to the launch.

'Home, my young man. Terra firma. The good soil of Wales under our feet!'

The able seaman at the wheel smiled mechanically, and muttered under his breath. Griffiths and I clung to the side of the launch and looked back at *Cassandra*. She was being drawn into the darker grey of the night, her lights the only indication of her shape and bulk. I though of the fire-power nesting in her belly and the pressed white shirts of the party. Then, in her stern, I caught sight of a movement. It was a blur of blue, like a loosed blue feather. Audrey's blue dress. She was on deck, looking out towards our launch, or the town, or just the sea, perhaps. I thought of that high, sheltered English accent, the world they'd

77

inherited, she and her sailor boys. I imagined, close-up, the line of her back and her lips forming the words yes and no.

'God bless her, and all who sail in her,' declared Griffiths. Then he unzipped and pissed into the sea. I joined him and we streamed the night's waste away. I think there was no rancour or stupidity or insult intended by either of us then. I looked up and pointed to the smiling moon.

'Yes, a fine night. Life's not all shit. A memorable night,' he said, stretching his arms upwards and belching.

The last words I heard him say on that occasion.

For further reading

Poetry
Album (Christopher Davies, 1974)
Preparations (Gomer, 1980)
Letting Go (Poetry Wales Press, 1983)
Selected Poems (Seren, 1986)
The Last Candles (Seren, 1989)
Taken for Pearls (Seren, 1993)
War Voices (Seren, 1995)
The Arches (with John Digby, Seren, 1998)
Heaven's Gate (Seren, 2001)

Anthologies edited
Love from Wales (with Siân James, Seren, 1991)
Coal (Seren, 1997)
The Poetry of Pembrokeshire (Seren, 1989)
The Poetry of Snowdonia (Seren, 1989)

Literary Criticism
Dannie Abse (Writers of Wales, University of Wales Press, 1985)
Wales: the Imagined Nation (ed. Poetry Wales Press, 1986)
How to Study Modern Poetry (Macmillan, 1990)
The Art of Seamus Heaney (ed. Seren, 1994)
How Poets Work (ed. Seren, 1996)

Art Criticism
Welsh Painters Talking (ed. Seren, 1997)
Welsh Artists Talking (ed. Seren, 2000)
Related Twilights by Josef Herman (ed. Seren, 2002)

Autobiography
Essay in Sam Adams (ed.), *Seeing Wales Whole: Essays on the Literature of Wales in honour of Meic Stephens* (University of Wales Press, 1998)

Images of Wales

The Corgi Series covers, no.7
'The Rape of the Sabine Women' by Ceri Richards; 1948; oil on canvas (Private Collection: Image used by permission of the Ceri Richards family & Estate)

Ceri Richards (1903-71) was the outstanding Welsh painter of the 20th century. Born in Dunvant to a working class, but highly cultured family, he absorbed the elements of music and poetry, in both languages. After student years at Swansea College of Art and the Royal College he became a tutor and artist based in London. He taught in Cardiff College of Art during the war years. He was greatly influenced by the poetry of both Dylan Thomas and Vernon Watkins and continued to spend much time on the Gower as a neighbour of Watkins. He painted and produced graphic art inspired by and in memory of both poets. He worked in series of themes, including the Sabine Theme in 1948 and 1949, and worked on monumental series based on Debussy's *Cathédrale engloutie* and Beethoven's piano compositions. His life and work was the subject of one of John Ormond's famous BBC films. A major retrospective was held in the Tate Gallery in 1980 and in the National Gallery of Wales in Cardiff in 2002. Mel Gooding's *Ceri Richards* was published in 2002.

Tony Curtis has written extensively on art in Wales and has a particular interest in Ceri Richards. The painting used on the cover is the subject of one of the poems published here.